GREECE
A SPIRITED INDEPENDENCE

DISCOVERING our HERITAGE

By Diana Spyropulos

DILLON PRESS, INC.
Minneapolis, Minnesota 55415

Acknowledgments

The author wishes to thank the following people for their assistance for providing information or photographs: Diana and Andreas Stavropoulos, Chrisoula Antonopoulos, Ismene Vassiliou, Dimitri and Chrisoula Stavrapoulos, Potoula and Apostole Stavrapoulos, Tasia Tragakou and Tonia Tragakou-Christothoulou, Peter Demos, Katherine Spyropulos, Peggy and George Lebberes, John and Betty Spyropulos, Valerie Dahlberg, Carrin Schechter, Emily McLennon, Amalia Poulos, Pauline Mouroulis, Caroline Nowell Cardamis, Lorraine A. Morash, Irene Tsasapatanis, the Parlitsis family, the family of Father Christos Papachristou, Father Theodore Bagnaleas, Mr. Velonis (Greek National Tourist Board), Lucille Pfeifer, Maggie Yates (Katonah Library, New York), Dimitri Gemelos, George Dardavilas, Yiorgo Chouliaras (Greek Press and Information Office), Nicos Nicolidakis (Greek Consulate's Office for Educational Affairs), AP/Wide World, Robert Fried, and Margot Granitsas. Cover photo by Robert Fried.

Library of Congress Cataloging-in-Publication Data

Spyropulos, Diana.
    Greece : a spirited independence / by Diana Spyropulos.
      p.   cm. — (Discovering our heritage)
    Bibliography: p.
    Includes index.
    Summary: Describes the history of civilization in Greece, its blend of religion and mythology, and how modern life there has been shaped by its past.
    ISBN 0-87518-311-5 (lib. bdg.)
    1. Greece—Civilization—Juvenile literature. [1. Greece—Civilization.] I. Title. DF741.S85 1990
    949.5—dc19   85-25412
                                           CIP
                                         AC

Dillon Press, Inc., 242 Portland Avenue South
Minneapolis, Minnesota 55415

Printed in the United States of America
1 2 3 4 5 6 7 8 9 10 99 98 97 96 95 94 93 92 91 90

Contents

Fast Facts about Greece

Official Name: *Elliniki Dimokratia* ("The Hellenic Republic").

Capital: Athens.

Location: Southeastern corner of Europe; it borders Bulgaria, Yugoslavia, and Albania to the north; the Aegean Sea and Turkey to the east; the Mediterranean Sea to the south; and the Ionian Sea to the west.

Area: Approximately 50,950 square miles (approximately 130,900 square kilometers). *Greatest distances:* north-south—365 miles (587 kilometers); east-west—345 miles (555 kilometers). *Coastline:* more than 9,300 miles (14,880 kilometers), including islands.

Elevation: *Highest*—9,570 feet (2,917 meters) above sea level at Mount Olympus. *Lowest*—sea level at the coasts.

Population *(Estimated 1989 population)*: 10,000,000.

Form of Government: Republic. *Head of government*— Prime Minister.

Important Products: Olives and olive products, cotton, grapes, lemons, tobacco, goats, sheep, clothing, textiles, processed foods, bauxite, chromite, lignite.

Basic Unit of Money: Drachma.

Major Language: Greek.

Major Religion: 95 percent Greek Orthodox.

Flag: The Greek flag has nine alternating stripes of blue and white. In its upper left-hand corner, a white cross appears on a blue background. The cross symbolizes the Greek Orthodox Church, the blue stands for the sea and the sky, and the white means purity.

National Anthem: "Imnos pros tin Eleftherian" ("The Hymn to Liberty").

Major Holidays: St. Basil's Day—January 1; Feast of the Epiphany—January 6; Independence Day—March 25; St. Constantine's Day—May 21; Easter—date varies; Christmas—December 25. In addition, many festivals and saints' name days are celebrated locally.

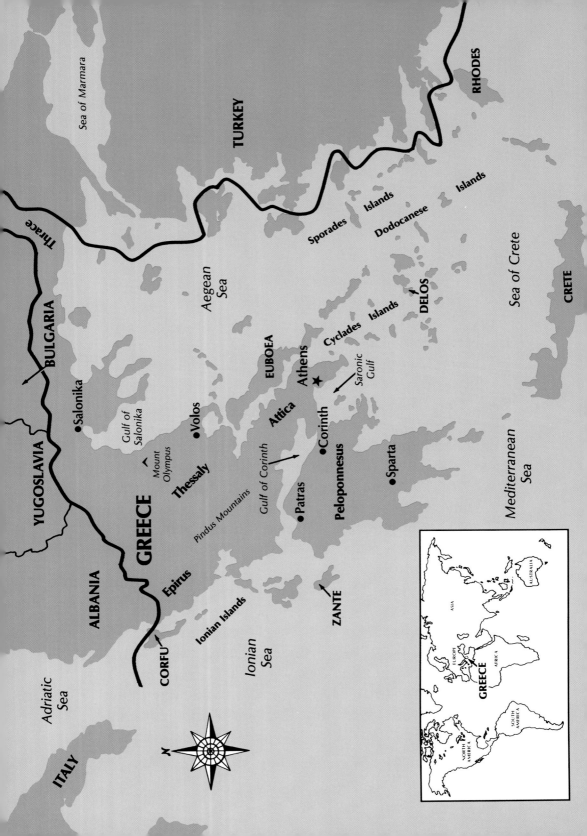

1. Land of Mountains and Seas

Imagine a land of sparkling blue seas, rugged mountains, and beautiful wildflowers. Imagine a country where 2,500-year-old monuments rise next to video arcades and fast-food restaurants. In Greece, you don't have to imagine these things—they are a part of life.

Greece is a small peninsula in the southeastern corner of Europe. The entire country could fit within the American state of Georgia. Since ancient times, its soil has been poor and stony, unable to support all of its people. Yet this hard land was the birthplace of Western civilization.

Greece is bordered on the north by Bulgaria, Yugoslavia, and Albania, and on the east by the Aegean Sea and Turkey. The country's shores are washed by the Ionian Sea on the west, and by the Mediterranean Sea on the south. In fact, wherever you stand in Greece, you are almost always in sight of mountains, and never more than 85 miles (137 kilometers) from the sea.

The mountains and the seas have always played an important role in shaping Greek character, industry, and history. At one time, mountains were barriers to travel and communications. Greek mountain roads were crooked, stony, and steep, so mountain people did not com-

A seaside village on the island of Santorini.

municate much with communities in other areas.

The seas, on the other hand, made communication easy for people in the coastal areas. They made contact early in their history with the peoples of Africa, Asia, and Europe. But these Greeks did not explore the seas just to trade or settle new colonies. They were attracted by the thrill of the unknown, and by the opportunity to learn from other cultures.

Because so much of the country is surrounded by water, the fishing industry is very important to the Greek economy. More than two hundred species of fish are found in Greek waters, among them bass, swordfish, cod, and mackerel. Boat building and net mending are also common activities in Greece's ports and coves. Many young people still make their living fishing and sailing, just as their ancestors did. Often, parents and children work side by side, throwing their nets into the sea until the sun goes down.

Maritime trade is also an important business in Greece. Greece's fleet of cargo vessels is the third largest in the world. Piraeus, in the Saronic Gulf near Athens, is Greece's most important port.

Agriculture is the chief occupation of the Greek villages today, just as it was thousands of years ago. Wheat, apricots, figs, olives, grapes, and tobacco are important farm products. Tobacco makes up about one-third of Greece's agricultural exports. The country is famous for its olives and olive oil, too, which are used all over the world.

Farms in Greece are usually small, with an average of only 8 acres (3.2 hectares) each. These farms are almost always passed down from generation to generation within a family.

People in rural areas live on the plains or in the mountains. Although most of the nation's land is stony, Greece does have five fertile plains which are excellent for farming. Because of modern farming methods, life has improved for the plains dwellers in the past decade.

Terraced fields rise up the stony slopes of Greece's mountains.

The mountain farmers are not as lucky as those who live on the plains. In spite of progress, farmers still find it takes much hard work to make a living from the mountain soil. Farming villages are usually located on a slope or hillside, and sometimes on steep cliffs. This leaves every possible flat area for planting crops.

The mountains and the seas divide Greece into eight regions. The mainland regions are called Thrace, Macedonia, Epirus, the Peloponnesus, and Central Greece. The three island regions are the Ionian Islands, the Aegean Islands, and Crete—the largest Greek island.

The Greek Islands

About one-fifth of the area of Greece is made up of islands. There are more than 1,400 of them scattered in the three seas. Some are wooded; some are rocky, dry, and treeless; and others are tropical or volcanic. Only about 160 of the Greek islands are inhabited. Visitors from all over the world, including the Greeks themselves, come to explore them.

The Ionian Islands, in the Ionian Sea, are to the west of mainland Greece. Unlike most of the country, these islands have a mild climate and plenty of rainfall. While temperatures in the rest of Greece can soar as high as 100°F (38°C) in the summer, island temperatures are usually between 80°F and 90°F (27°C to 32°C).

Agriculture, fishing, and tourism are major industries in the Ionian Islands. The largest and most populated of these are Zante, Cephalonia, and Corfu. Corfu, the northernmost island, is known for its gently rolling hills, beautiful old villages, tiny churches, and forests of olive and cypress trees. Countless wild plants bloom all year long. The people of Corfu are known for their appreciation of music, and mandolins and guitars are popular instruments.

The Aegean Islands lie east of the mainland in the Aegean Sea. They are rocky, have little rainfall, and are not good for farming. Most of the uninhabited Aegean Islands are divided into four groups—the Saronic, the Dodocanese, the Sporades, and the Cyclades, which means "circle" in Greek.

The islands in the Cyclades group are named because they form a circle around the sacred island of Delos. According to Greek mythology, the god Apollo was born on Delos.

The island of Tinos is a well-known part of the Cyclades group, too. It is home to a church named the Panayia Evangelistria. Inside the church is a religious painting of the Angel of the Annunciation speaking to the Virgin Mary. According to legend, it was painted by Saint Luke. Twice a year, pilgrims from all over Greece travel to this church to offer their prayers to Mary. Many sick people claim to have been healed there.

Delos lies in the center of a ring formed by the Cyclades Islands.

Crete

The third grouping of Greek islands is actually just one island—Crete. Located in the Mediterranean Sea, Crete is the largest of the Greek islands. Folk traditions are still a part of everyday life here, and Cretan weddings and other gatherings are among the liveliest in Greece. Singers entertain the crowds with lyrics from *Erotokritos*, Crete's national epic poem, or with the

Mantinades, a type of rhymed poem that is made up as it goes along.

Farmers and Shepherds

In the northeastern corner of mainland Greece is Thrace, bordered by Turkey to the east and Bulgaria to the north. Thrace is best known for its tobacco products.

Macedonia, to the west of Thrace, is the largest region in Greece and has the best agriculture. It stretches south from the Yugoslav border to include Mount Olympus—legendary home of the gods, and the highest mountain in Greece—and west from the Aegean Sea to the Pindus Mountains. Wheat, oats, cotton, and tobacco are grown in this region.

Salonika, the second largest city in Greece, is in Macedonia. It has been a busy seaport and commercial center since 315 B.C. Products such as textiles and tobacco are manufactured and processed in plants outside the city. Besides being a city of commerce, Salonika has many museums and churches filled with beautiful examples of religious art.

On the western side of the Pindus Mountains, extending to the Gulf of Corinth, lies Epirus. Epirus is a mountainous region, and many of its people are shepherds, just as they have been for centuries. Others work in the area's aluminum factories or bauxite mines.

The Peloponnesus

The Peloponnesus is a large peninsula in southern Greece with rugged mountains and many small villages. It is almost separated from the mainland by the Corinth Canal. It is a dry and rocky region, and with the exception of olives, crops do not grow well here.

The Peloponnesus is one of the most historically famous parts of Greece. Ancient temples still stand in the ruins of Corinth, Olympia—where the first Olympics were held—and many other towns.

Central Greece

Central Greece includes the region of Thessaly, the large island of Euboea near the east coast, and Attica. Many of Euboea's residents are shepherds. Thessaly supplies Greece with large amounts of cotton and wheat.

At the northwestern edge of Thessaly stand giant rocks which have been twisted into odd shapes. Geologists say these formations, called *Meteora*, were carved out millions of years ago when the land was covered by the sea. Old monastaries, filled with treasures of religious art, perch eerily on the peaks of the Meteora.

Attica, to the south of Thessaly, is one of the driest, most barren areas in all of Greece. Greece's capital, Athens, lies near the southern tip of Attica.

The ruins of the Parthenon stand atop the Acropolis *in Athens.*

Athens is considered the heart of Greece. Although the land around the city is poor, Athens is the country's cultural, artistic, and political center.

Ancient Athens was built around a flat-topped hill, the *Acropolis*. The Parthenon, a large, marble temple dedicated to the protector of the city, Athena, was its most famous temple. Parts of the Parthenon still stand today.

On the northern slope of the Acropolis is the Plaka.

The Plaka is a mixture of tiny, pastel-colored houses and narrow, twisting lanes. No map or guide is needed here because the streets always lead up!

At the foot of the Acropolis is the *agora*, or marketplace. In ancient Greece, it was not only a place for shopping and trading, but also an exciting place to meet people from all over the world. Sailors, politicians, peasants, and philosophers gathered there each day.

Today, many Athenians still like to meet near the site of the agora and at other places in the city. They sit with their friends and talk at sidewalk cafes. Like their ancestors, most Athenians enjoy questioning everything and discussing world politics, economics, or culture.

Modern Athens is a lively, noisy, crowded city. People from all over Greece come to Athens to find work or a more exciting life than they could have in rural areas. The cultural activities and busy atmosphere are as attractive to Greeks as they are to tourists—one of the reasons why more than 8 million people visited Greece in 1987 alone. Hotels, restaurants, and other tourist-related businesses employ more Greeks than any other industry.

When Athens became the capital of Greece in 1834, the city was a collection of run-down houses with a population of only 5,000 people. Today, almost four of every ten Greeks—about 4 million people—live there.

One of the many monuments that crowd Athens is

the former Royal Palace in Syntagma Square, which has been the seat of Parliament since 1933. Since Greece gained its independence from Turkey in 1827, it has experienced various types of governments. It has had constitutional monarchies, dictatorships, and republics.

Today, Greece is a republic, with three major political parties: the New Democracy, the Pan Hellenic Socialist Movement, and the Communist party. The government is made up of a president, a parliament, and a prime minister. The president, whose role is mainly ceremonial, is head of state and is elected by the parliament. The parliament is the lawmaking part of the government and is elected by the Greek people. Through the decisions of parliament, the president may declare war and ally Greece with other countries.

The prime minister is the most powerful person in the Greek government, and leads the majority party in parliament. Andreas Papandreou of the Socialist party was prime minister from 1981 to 1989. Then a temporary government took over after Papandreou lost an election due to scandals in the government.

Greece is a land that is as harsh as it is beautiful. To survive there has always required courage and intelligence. The land of Greece has created a practical, yet poetic people who know how to take pleasure in small things, and to make the most of each moment.

Mountain peaks ring Athens, the capital of Greece.

2. *A Sense of* Philotemo

Sophocles, an ancient Greek playwright, wrote, "The world is full of wonders, but none more wonderful than man." The modern Greek, like her ancestors, shares this delight in other people. It is one of the qualities that best describes the Greek character.

When you first meet a Greek, he or she will usually want to know all about you. Visitors are asked where they come from, what they study in school, and what they like to do for fun.

The Greek people are also well known for their hospitality. Hospitality, or making a guest feel welcome, is taken very seriously in Greece. It is a part of what makes up a Greek's *philotemo*, or a sense of honor and self-respect. Whether a stranger comes from the next village or half the world away, that person is met with warmth and kindness. A visitor to a Greek home between meals will traditionally be offered a thick fruit jam, a pastry, or a soft chewy candy called *loukoumi*. Strangers are treated as if they were guests. In fact, *xenos*, the Greek word for "strangers," also means "guests."

Greek character varies depending on which part of the country a person is from. Mountain farmers are

A mountain farmer on Crete.

known for being reserved and serious in nature. They are also said to be brave and self-reliant, meaning they do not depend on other people. These characteristics may be formed by living in isolated villages and trying to make a living from the stony soil. Despite difficult living conditions, Greeks in mountain villages are known for their love of music. Many do not need a special occasion to dance or sing. Their songs, which begin slowly and sadly, end joyfully. Mountain farmers are considered to be the backbone of Greece, a source of many of the nation's leaders. Many politicians, diplomats, doctors, artists, and teachers come from mountain farming families.

Unlike their mountain cousins, Greeks who live near the sea have a reputation for being extremely open and cheerful. Perhaps it is because they have had more opportunity to meet people from other cultures. Their music, which is generally light-hearted and quick in tempo, shows their appreciation of life.

Family and Friends

Most Greeks are not shy about showing their feelings, especially among family and friends. They cry openly when they are sad and laugh out loud when they are happy. Greek parents are usually very affectionate toward their children. They hug them, fuss over them, and call them pet names such as *matia mou* (my eyes), *poulaki mou* (my little bird), and *chriso mou* (my golden one).

In addition to having a strong family life, most Greeks are very sociable. They enjoy going out with friends to restaurants, cafes, and for long walks under the stars. Greeks are also said to be among the greatest

Cafes in villages and cities are meeting spots for many Greeks.

talkers in the world. Often, they talk more loudly than people in the United States or Western Europe do. To a visitor, it may look as if they are having an argument when they may just be trying to decide where to have coffee.

In villages and small towns, the *peripato*, or evening stroll, has played an important part in life for centuries. Between seven and nine o'clock in the evening, families head for the town square or harbor. The strollers greet everyone they meet, no matter how often they have seen each other that day. Sometimes they pause to chat. The peripato plays an important role in social life, match-making, and even business dealings. This custom holds communities together in villages and small towns.

Religion, too, is important to life, especially in small towns. Ninety-five percent of the Greek people belong to the Greek Orthodox Church. Though most Greeks don't go to church on a regular basis, religion has an influence on everyday life. When things such as spring planting or the building of a new house are begun, the local priest is called to offer his blessings. When some Greeks have a problem, they will light a candle to their favorite saint and ask for help.

The Greek Individual

Although Greeks are said to be very friendly as a people, they are known for being independent, too. At the very center of the traditional Greek outlook is the belief in the individual worth of each Greek woman or man. Even the most terrible poverty does not destroy a Greek's sense of self-worth. Keeping one's pride through any hardship, and respecting the pride of others, is an-other part of what makes up a Greek's philotemo.

Most Greeks are very proud of their independence. They often question and sometimes disrespect authority.

Two girls on their way to a political party just before elections.

This attitude can be traced to ancient Greece, when many people laughed at the government and even the gods.

A Greek's individualism is expressed in a love of argument and discussion. A large number of people in Greece enjoy talking about politics. Discussions about the government and its leaders take place on trains, buses, and planes, and in homes, cafes, and restaurants—almost anywhere you can think of. Sometimes, a discussion can turn into an argument. Some people get so angry that they refuse to speak to each other for days!

Election time is always exciting in Greece. People hang their party's flag outside the window of their home or from their car, and drivers with the same party flags usually beep at each other. Greek children, too, sometimes have strong opinions of their own about politics. It is not uncommon for a child of four or five years old to call out to a friend on the street, "Who are you voting for, my friend?"

When Greeks take time to criticize their faults, they usually say that their strong independence makes it hard for them to work together. Often, nothing gets accomplished because everyone is busy arguing. Fortunately, the tradition of becoming a small shopkeeper, farmer, fisherman, or artisan allows many Greeks to be what makes them happiest—their own boss.

Lovers of Adventure

Few modern Greeks resemble their tall, blonde ancestors. Most Greeks are dark-skinned, dark-haired, and short by North American standards. But the ancient and modern Greeks resemble each other in spirit. They share the same love of adventure, the same respect for others, and a strong sense of liberty.

The Greek's love of liberty is often expressed in

demotiki, or folk music. One of the best known folk songs is called "The Zolongo Dance." It is based on an event that happened on December 23, 1803. By this time, most of Greece had been conquered by Turkey and under its control for more than three hundred years. One of the last unoccupied villages was Souli, in the region of Epirus.

The men of the village were away fighting the Turks. When the women learned that the men had been killed and the Turks were advancing on the village, they decided they would rather die than become slaves of their conquerors. It is said that they joined hands and did a chain dance off the cliff of Zolongo.

Schoolchildren learn about the women of Souli in their history classes. Over the years, sculptors and painters have portrayed the women of Souli and their chain dance. Even now, the sad lyrics and the beautiful music are very special to many Greeks.

Demotiki music describes a variety of people— farmers, shepherds, fishermen, sailors, wild young men, and proud young women. Harp-like lyres are used in demotiki music, as are bagpipes made of goatskin, clarinets, and all kinds of wooden flutes.

Bouzouki music is the popular music of Greece. It can be sad and happy at the same time. Bouzouki songs are often about a man who is tough on the outside, but really very sensitive at heart. He is usually in love with a

woman he considers a kind of goddess, someone he puts on a pedestal. Many Greeks love to dance traditional dances solo to bouzouki music.

Mikis Theodorakis and Manos Hadjidakis are among Greece's most famous and gifted composers. Their music combines bouzouki and folk music. Both composers have set the words of ancient and modern poets to music.

The Music of Words

In ancient times, poetry was almost a second religion to many Greeks, and poets were highly respected. "The poet," said the philosopher Socrates, "is a light and winged and holy thing."

The earliest surviving works of Greek literature are the *Iliad* and the *Odyssey*, by Homer. These long poems, or epics, are considered among the greatest ever written. Homer told of the exciting adventures of gods and goddesses, of their faults and virtues. Many experts think that if not for the works of Homer, little would be known about very early Greek history.

Two modern Greek poets have won the Nobel Prize for literature—George Seferis in 1963, and Odysseus Elytis in 1979. Seferis's poetry is usually very serious in tone. It is about the dignity and sorrows in people's lives. Elytis's poetry is often joyous and carefree. The

Musicians perform at a festival in Metsovo.

images he describes are often filled with hope for the future.

One of the most beloved characters of modern Greek literature is the main character in *Zorba the Greek*, a novel by Nikos Kazantzakis. Zorba is known for his zest for life, for being unashamed to show his feelings, and for his wisdom and sense of humor—all the characteristics admired by the Greek people. *Zorba the Greek* is one of the world's best-known novels and has been translated into thirty-four languages.

All over Greece, one finds the same religion, language, and customs. In spite of generations of wars, invasions, and occupations, the Greek people have kept and treasured their customs and heritage. Throughout their history, their strong sense of national and personal pride has helped them survive as a people.

3. A Great Adventure

Greek history began about five thousand years ago on Crete, one of the largest islands in the Mediterranean Sea. Historians call the civilization that developed there the Minoan culture, after King Minos, the legendary ruler of Crete.

The Minoans were explorers and traders. Through their travels, they spread their art, pottery, and jewelry as far as Egypt, Asia Minor—now Turkey—and Mesopotamia, which covered parts of today's Turkey, Syria, and Iraq.

They were also a peaceful people who lived in cities, small towns, and villages. Farmers earned a good living from the soil, and wealthy people lived in palaces or on estates. Some lived in the king's court at the palace of Knossos.

This huge, brightly-colored palace covered six acres (2.4 hectares) on northern Crete near Iraklion, the present capital. The palace was highly advanced for its time. It had offices, storerooms, workshops, and living quarters. Some parts of the palace were five stories high. When archaeologists uncovered the palace in the early 1900s, they even discovered the remains of a type of plumbing system.

A mural in the palace of Knossos shows young people taking part in the ancient sport of bull leaping.

Mycenaeans and Trojans

The Minoans were the most important culture in the Aegean area until about 1450 B.C. At that time, it is thought that the Mycenaeans took control.

The Mycenaeans are named for Mycenaea, a powerful town that developed in the Peloponnesus region of mainland Greece in 2000 B.C. The Mycenaeans were sailors and warriors, and conquered the Minoans easily. They were greatly influenced by the Minoans, though, and from them learned to make fine pottery and metal-work, as well as how to build strong, stone buildings. The Mycenaeans also adapted the Minoan writing system to the Greek language.

In 1200 B.C., the Mycenaeans fought a war with the Trojans, a people from Asia Minor. For many years, historians believed that the Trojan War, described in Homer's *Iliad*, was a myth. But in 1870, a German archaeologist uncovered the remains of Troy. Now most experts agree the war was actually waged.

The Trojan War began when Paris, the son of a Trojan king, fell in love with Helen, wife of the king of Sparta, a powerful Greek village. Paris kidnapped Helen and returned with her to Troy.

Menelaus, Helen's husband, asked his brother, King Agamemnon of Mycenaea, for help in getting Helen back. Agamemnon agreed, and with the support of the other Greek kings, they marched to Troy.

However, the walls surrounding the city of Troy were so well defended that the Greeks could not get into the city. For ten years, the Trojans and the Greeks fought each other.

Finally, the Greeks came up with a plan they felt sure would trick the Trojans. They built a giant wooden horse and hid most of the soldiers inside it. Then they gave the horse to the Trojans as a token of peace. The Trojans accepted the gift, and brought it inside the city

Ruins of ancient Greek temples such as this one dot the Greek landscape.

walls. That night, the Greek soldiers climbed out of the horse, opened the city gates to let the remaining soldiers in, and defeated the Trojans.

Shortly after this battle, the Mycenaean culture was destroyed. Some historians think the Mycenaeans were conquered by a group of people from northern Greece.

The four hundred years following the disappearance of the Mycenaeans is called the Dark Age. During this period, the advanced communities of the Mycenaeans and the Minoans broke down, and Greeks lived in small, isolated villages. All knowledge of writing systems was lost, and stories, legends, and histories were related through songs and oral poetry.

After 800 B.C., Greeks began to write again, and people began to record poetry, history, and scientific discoveries. It was at this time that Homer is thought to have put much of Greece's oral poetry in the *Iliad* and the *Odyssey*.

Toward the end of the Dark Age, Greek communities called city-states began to develop. City-states were a collection of individual cities surrounded by farms and villages. The nobility, or upper class, governed the city-states, and owned almost all the best land.

Because there was too little land for the people of Greece, the city-states were often fighting over borders. Some city-states, such as Athens and Sparta, grew very powerful. Sparta was known for the fierceness of its people. Both boys and girls were trained to fight in battle, and one of the most admired qualities in a Spartan was physical fitness.

One place in which Spartans could test their physical abilities was at the Olympic Games. Beginning in 776 B.C., the games were held every four years at Olympia in honor of Zeus, king of all the Greek gods. The Olympics drew people from all over the Greek world. Even before the official games would begin, singers, poets, musicians, and speakers would compete for prizes, while philosophers and politicians debated each other.

Even the Olympic Games, however, could not keep peace among the Greek peoples. Between 700 and 500 B.C., Greek farmers, merchants, and slaves were beginning to demand better living conditions and a greater influence in the government. But the nobles who ruled the city-states refused to give up power. Soon, small revolutions broke out in which the rulers were forced out of power. Dictators took their place at first, but were soon replaced by an *oligarchy*. An oligarchy is a form of government run by a few wealthy people.

In 500 B.C., the idea of democracy was introduced in Athens. An Athenian named Cleisthenes made a constitution, gave voting rights to some of the people, and created a 500-member government council which was open to all Athenians. For the first time, people had a say in what went on in their community.

In about 494 B.C., Athenians rushed to the aid of Greek colonies in Asia Minor that were being invaded by Persia (now called Iran). To punish the Athenians for their actions, the Persians invaded Greece in 490 B.C. The Greek city-states joined forces and defeated the Persians at the Battle of Marathon, even though the Greeks were outnumbered two to one. The Persians invaded again about ten years later. They conquered Athens, much of which they burned down. But in 479 B.C., they were defeated by the Greek forces. As a result of this war, Athens became the most powerful city-state, with Sparta a close second. The defeat of the Persians left the Athenians filled with pride, and free to concentrate more on culture than on war.

The Golden Age

During the fifth century B.C., for a period of almost fifty years, Greece entered its Golden Age. This was the time of Greece's greatest achievements in art, literature, philosophy, and government. The man whom many think is chiefly responsible for this was a statesman named Pericles. Pericles wanted to make Athens a great center for culture. He set aside sixty official holidays so that citizens could attend drama, dance, and poetry festivals. He also helped create a feeling of freedom in the people, which helped many fully develop their talents.

During the Golden Age, the Parthenon was built in Athens to honor the city's patroness, the goddess Athena. It took almost twenty years to build the white marble temple on top of the Acropolis.

Also during the Golden Age, playwrights such as Sophocles and Euripides wrote some of their greatest works. At festival time each spring, Athenians would crowd into the theater of Dionysius, an open-air theater built below the Acropolis, to watch their dramas and comedies being performed.

Education, too, was important at this time. The great philosopher Socrates began voicing his ideas in the streets and marketplace of Athens. He believed that evil was caused by lack of knowledge, and that people should try to learn all they could about the world and the people around them. One of Socrates' pupils was Plato, who in turn taught the philosopher Aristotle.

By this time, the Athenians were firm believers in democracy. Every citizen—meaning all free men more than eighteen years old—had a seat on the popular assembly, which made the decisions about how to run the city. The assembly met every ten days, and most citizens were eager to take part in the process. The Greeks had a word for a citizen who did not want to have a say in the government—*idiotes*. In English, this word means "idiot"!

In 431 B.C., the Golden Age ended when fighting

broke out between Athens and Sparta. Called the Peloponnesian War, it lasted almost thirty years. By the time Sparta had won, Athens had lost many of its greatest thinkers, soldiers, and writers.

Philip and Alexander

In 338 B.C., King Philip of Macedonia conquered Sparta and the rest of Greece, uniting all the city-states into one kingdom. Philip planned to invade Persia next, but he died before he could.

Philip's son, Alexander, became king of Greece in 336 B.C. He was twenty years old. The young king had been taught by Aristotle, who had given Alexander a love for Greek poetry, art, and philosophy. Alexander had been influenced greatly by the *Iliad*, and dreamed of adventures such as those described in the epic poem.

Shortly after Alexander became king of Greece, he and his army went to war with Persia, fulfilling his father's dream. In ten years, Alexander controlled the entire empire. Soon, he stretched the Greek world to the farthest boundaries of Persia, north to Russia, east to India, and south to Egypt. There, he founded the city of Alexandria.

The period following Alexander's death is known as the Hellenistic Age. Greek culture continued to influence the lands Alexander had conquered, and Alexandria

Alexander the Great.

became a center of great learning. It was in Alexandria that Eristratos, the physician, discovered how blood circulates through the body, and Archimedes discovered the principle of volume.

The Roman Empire

In 146 B.C., Greece was conquered by Rome. As a part of the Roman Empire, the country was influenced by Christianity. Under Roman rule, Greek city-states grew weak because the Romans did not allow them any military or political power.

In A.D. 395, the Roman Empire was divided in two, and Greece became a part of the East Roman Empire. It soon became known as the Byzantine Empire.

The capital of this vast nation was Constantinople, known today as Istanbul, Turkey. Like Alexandria, Constantinople was Greek, and was a center of learning and culture. It had many excellent universities and libraries.

Constantinople was founded by Emperor Constantine I, whom many people believe is the founder of the Greek Orthodox religion. He built great churches and appointed several bishops to spread the Christian faith throughout the empire and surrounding lands.

By 325, Christianity had become the state religion of the Byzantine Empire. The ancient Greek religions were outlawed, and churches dedicated to the new faith were built in Athens. The temples which had been built for the Greek gods and goddesses were converted into Christian shrines. Even the Parthenon was turned into a church of the Virgin Mary.

Many Greeks welcomed Christianity. Others secretly worshipped their gods and goddesses for many years after Greece had officially become Christian.

During the Byzantine period, Greek trade, agriculture, and industry grew. Also, the Romans borrowed from Greek culture, and spread their art, religions, philosophy, and life-style throughout the empire.

However, because Greece was at the very frontier of the Byzantine Empire, it was hard to protect. During this period, Greece was invaded many times by peoples from all over Europe.

The Byzantine Empire finally collapsed on May 29, 1453, when Turkish armies arrived in Constantinople. It had lasted longer than any other empire in European history.

4. A New Greece

By 1460, the Turks had won control of mainland Greece. Some Greeks had fled to other parts of Europe rather than live under Turkish rule. Of the Greeks who remained, many never stopped fighting for their freedom. In spite of such resistance, the Turks ruled Greece for almost four hundred years.

The centuries under Turkish rule were hard for the freedom-loving Greeks. Modern Greeks still consider this period the worst in their history. The Parthenon, a national Greek symbol, was converted into a Moslem mosque, or temple. To prevent rebellions, the Turks outlawed public meetings. Also, in the early days of Turkish rule, boys aged six to nine were rounded up every four years. The strongest 20 percent of these were taken to Constantinople to become members of the Turkish sultan's special guard.

No matter how they suffered, the Greeks did not lose their pride. After many unsuccessful rebellions, they revolted again in 1821. On March 25, Archbishop Germanos of Patras, a leader of the Greek Orthodox Church, raised a homemade flag with the Greek cross on a blue background, defying Turkish law. The revolution had begun.

Bouboulina, heroine of the Greek revolution against the Turks.

Independence at Last

The revolution was fought on land and at sea. Greek fighters called *klephtes* came down from bases in the mountains to win back land in southern and central Greece. They also regained some islands. The Turks, along with their Egyptian allies, took back much of this territory in 1825, but the revolution continued.

Meanwhile, Greek shipowners were turning their

vessels into a navy of fighting ships. A wealthy Greek shipowner named Bouboulina joined the fight and became a heroine of the revolution. With great courage, she commanded her own ship, the *Agamemnon*. Later, she fought on land with Kolokotronis, a famous klepht general.

In 1827, Great Britain, France, and Russia agreed to help Greece fight. They sent a combined navy that defeated the Turks. The next year Russia declared war on Turkey. The Turkish armies, along with their ally, Egypt, pulled out of Greece in 1829.

Newly independent Greece was a tiny state of fewer than 800,000 people. Its land area included the central mainland, the Peloponnesus region, and several nearby islands—about half the size of Greece today. Several million Greeks lived in Turkey, or on land controlled by the Turks. This created a desire for many Greeks for what they called the "Great Idea." This was a dream to unite all Greeks in the Mediterranean area into one state.

Greece's first government was set up by its allies, Britain, France, and Russia. They appointed Otto, crown prince of Bavaria, as king of Greece in 1833. Otto's reign was not popular with many Greeks, though, because he had almost unlimited powers. The Greek people staged a peaceful rebellion in 1844 and forced King Otto to accept a parliament and prime minister. In 1862, Otto was replaced by King George I, a ruler who believed in democracy. King George created a constitution that limited royal powers and gave a lot of power to an elected government.

The early years of Greek independence were marked by struggles to win back Greek lands still under foreign control. In 1863, the Ionian Islands were won back from Great Britain. In 1881, Thessaly was taken back, too.

The Balkan Wars of 1912 to 1913 were fought to free lands still under Turkey's control. After these wars, Greek territory almost doubled. The regions of Epirus, Macedonia, Crete, and most of the Aegean Islands were added to the Greek lands. Nearly 1.5 million Greeks were once again a part of Greece.

In 1910, a statesman from Crete, Eleftherios Venizelos, became prime minister of Greece. His social and economic reforms were so important that they transformed Greece into a modern country.

Prime Minister Venizelos was chiefly responsible for the building of hundreds of schools throughout Greece. He made education free—and required. He encouraged the arts, modernized the army, and founded the Bank of Greece as the country's national central bank.

In addition, Venizelos created large-scale draining projects in Macedonia and Thrace, which wiped out malaria from these regions. He passed laws protecting the rights of working women and minors, and revised

Eleftherios Venizelos.

the 1864 constitution. Venizelos added new laws to strengthen individual freedoms, property rights, and freedom of the press.

Many Greeks consider Venizelos to be the greatest prime minister in modern Greek history. His politics were responsible for doubling the area of Greece after the Balkan Wars. For many years, he succeeded in making parliament, the royalty, and the army cooperate instead of argue with each other.

World War I

World War I began in 1914, but Greece stayed neutral until 1917. At that time, it joined on the side of the allies against Germany, Bulgaria, and Turkey. When the war ended in 1918, Greece gained even more territory.

For the next seventeen years, even Venizelos could not keep peace in the Greek government. He was in and out of office eight times, and there were three different kings on the throne. Between 1923 and 1935, Greece was a republic. A president instead of a king was head of state. But in 1935, the royalists, supporters of the king, took power again and George II took the throne.

Venizelos lost an election held after King George II returned, and went to live in Paris shortly after. Just before he died in 1936, Venizelos showed his continuing concern for Greece by writing letters urging political opponents to cooperate with each other.

In 1936, King George II permitted General Ionannis Metaxas to establish a military dictatorship. Four years later, Greece became involved in World War II. On October 26, 1940, Italy invaded Greece after Metaxas had given the one-word reply, *"Oxi,"* ("No") to a series of demands made by Benito Mussolini, Italy's dictator. The Greeks showed their support of Metaxas's decision by arranging whitewashed stone on a bare hill in the Peloponnesus to form the word "OXI."

Greek soldiers during World War II.

The Greek army was successful in defending Greece from the Italian forces. Women and children carried ammunition for the soldiers over mountain trails too rugged even for donkeys. When the Greeks drove the Italians back across the Albanian border, they won the praise and attention of the world.

Soon, however, German forces joined the Italians in their attempt to invade Greece. Although the Greek armies put up a great fight, the powerful German army moved into Athens on April 27, 1941. The Athenians watched in sadness as the Greek flag was taken down from its pole on the Acropolis. In its place, the Germans raised the swastika, Germany's symbol while the Nazis ruled the country. It is said that the Greek soldier who was ordered to pull down the Greek flag later wrapped it around himself and jumped off a cliff.

During the Nazi occupation, the Greeks organized one of the best underground movements in Europe, fighting in secret against the German army. Many of these resistance fighters, as they were called, came to believe in communism. This is the economic and political theory that all goods and means of production should be owned by the state. In other words, there is no private property.

When World War II ended, the constitutional monarchy was restored, with both the king and the prime minister in power. The former resistance fighters, however, wanted to make Greece a communist country. When they tried to take control of the government, a civil war began that lasted from 1944 to 1949.

The civil war is one of the saddest chapters of Greek history. Many children were separated from their families by the war, and it was not uncommon for small children to be discovered starving in caves high up in the mountains.

After five years of fighting, the communist leaders

fled to other nations in Europe. The constitutional monarchy began trying to restore the country. More than a tenth of the population was homeless. Five thousand villages had been burned and abandoned, and the economy was destroyed.

Restoring Peace

Greek shipping helped finance the rebuilding of the country. Its fleet of cargo ships allowed Greece to trade with other countries, which helped the economy. Also, Greece received aid from the United States and British governments. The Greek people, too, received financial support from family members who had emigrated to foreign countries and now began sending money back to help their homeland. Over a period of several years, metal works, oil refineries, and chemical plants were built, and new jobs were created. Agriculture, the country's most important industry, also began to prosper. New international markets were found for fruit, tobacco, and other farm produce. Tourism, too, became a major industry as hotels and other tourist-related facilities were built all across Greece.

Major changes in Greek life-style occurred throughout the 1950s. Many Greeks moved from villages and small towns into big cities, such as Athens and Salonika. To house these people, apartment buildings were built.

During the 1960s, some Greeks began turning away from the old traditions in search of a more exciting life. Women began attending universities in higher numbers, young people began dating more than they had in the past, and there were fewer arranged marriages, even in the small villages.

Changes in Government

Greece remained a constitutional monarchy until 1967. King Paul had died in 1964, and his son, Constantine, had taken over as king. King Constantine and Prime Minister George Papandreou argued constantly over issues such as political power and control of the army. Finally, the king dismissed Papandreou in 1965. Many unsuccessful attempts to form and maintain a new government followed. At one point, Greece had four governments in two months. On April 21, 1967, a group of army colonels led by George Papadopoulos took power. King Constantine left the country.

For seven years, Greece was controlled by a military dictatorship. The government did not allow free speech, and placed bans on strikes and public meetings. Many Greeks protested. Soon, the prisons were filled with people who had spoken out against the government. In 1974, the military government was overthrown, and Greece was once again a republic.

A NATO Member

In April 1980, Greece and the United States signed an agreement for cooperation in science, education, technology, economics, and culture. The United States and Greece are also North America Treaty Organization (NATO) allies. Formed after World War II, NATO is an organization of many different countries which agree to defend each other in case of war.

In January 1981, Greece joined the European Economic Community (EEC), which allowed it to increase its exports to other European countries. Nearly 50 percent of all Greece's trade is with European countries. The United States, the Soviet Union, and countries of the Middle East are other important trading partners.

Throughout the 1980s, the Greek government worked toward the creation of a nuclear-free zone in the Balkans. An agreement between Albania, Romania, Yugoslavia, Bulgaria, and Greece would mean that all nuclear weapons would have to be removed from these countries.

Between 1981 and 1989, the Greek Socialist party, headed by Prime Minister Andreas Papandreou, ran Greece. The government improved health care, pensions, and women's rights. However, in 1989, political and financial frauds were discovered. The press, the Bank of Greece, and the parliament began investigating charges of theft and bribery relating to the disappearance of $210 million from the Bank of Crete. Investigators believed officials in the Socialist party were at fault.

In June 1989, elections were held to choose a new government. However, neither of Greece's three main political parties won a majority of the votes. A party must win a majority in order to form a government. The Communist party and the Conservative party formed a temporary government, which lasted until elections were held in November. Once again, neither party had a majority of votes. This time, all three parties agreed to form a temporary government.

Throughout its history, Greece has been the site of amazing discoveries in philosophy, art, and science. Yet today, Greece faces problems brought about by increasing industrialization and modernization. When large numbers of Greeks began moving to the cities in the 1950s and 1960s, overcrowding and pollution became a concern to many Greek people. Fumes from traffic, factories, and refineries are damaging the health of the people, as well as destroying some of the country's ancient monuments. To help reduce pollution in Athens, the government has passed driving bans. Drivers are allowed to operate their cars only on every other day, and everyone must use lead-free gasoline.

To make the cities less crowded, the government has been encouraging people to move back to small towns and villages. They have offered the people of Greece small business loans for building homes and developing farmland.

For five thousand years, the Greek people have struggled to overcome their problems. It has been a long and exciting history. Throughout this time, the people of Greece have not lost their spirit of adventure or their sense of philotemo. As they face the problems of the twentieth century, the people of the mountains and seas hope the adventure has just begun.

5. Gods, Goddesses, and Saints

Long ago, the ancient Greeks looked around in wonder at their strange and beautiful world. They were filled with questions about themselves and the whole universe. They answered these questions by creating stories—called myths.

Some Greek myths are meant to entertain, while others are meant to point out a moral (a lesson) or to explain human nature—why people do the things they do. Still other myths are about the adventures of goddesses, gods, and heroes. No one knows for certain who created the various myths, but we do know that the ancient poets traveled around the countryside, telling the myths in poems and songs at feasts and other special occasions. In this way, the myths spread from town to town. Eventually nearly all Greeks were worshiping the same gods and listening to the same stories. One story, the myth of creation, explains how the world was created. It also describes the birth of the gods.

Myth of Creation

Long before the gods appeared, the world was in a state of chaos, or emptiness. Gaea, or Mother Earth, came from this chaos. She soon gave birth to Uranus, the sky. Uranus was all set with sparkling stars and was beautiful to look at. The moment Gaea saw him, she fell in love with him. Uranus and Gaea became the parents of the Titans. The Titans were six powerful gods who had six powerful sisters, the Titanesses.

Soon Gaea gave birth to other sons. The Cyclops were huge monsters with one eye each. The other sons were terrible monsters, each with fifty heads and one hundred hands.

Uranus hated and feared all his children, so he seized them and flung them down into Tartarus, the deep, dark pit beneath the earth. Gaea became very angry at her husband's cruelty. She convinced one of the Titans, Cronus, to strike down Uranus with a sickle made of the hardest flint. Cronus struck his father and made him unable to have any more children. Then Cronus became ruler of the universe. He sat on the highest mountain and ruled over heaven and earth with his sister, Queen Rhea.

Cronus feared that one of his children would try to take the throne from him, just as he had taken it from his father. So each time Rhea gave birth, Cronus swallowed the newborn god or goddess. With all of his offspring trapped in his belly, Cronus felt secure as lord of the universe.

But Cronus's Titaness wife, Rhea, mourned the loss

of all her children. When she was expecting her sixth child, she asked Gaea for help in saving it. Gaea wrapped a stone in baby clothes and told Rhea to present it to Cronus. Cronus was fooled and swallowed the stone! Then Gaea helped Rhea secretly hide her son, Zeus, in a cave in Crete. Gentle nymphs, or fairies, tended him there.

Zeus grew quickly. Soon he came out of the cave a powerful young god, ready to fight with Cronus. The first thing he did was to trick his father into eating an herb that made him vomit Zeus's five brothers and sisters—Hestia, Demeter, Hera, Hades, and Poseidon.

Zeus and his brothers and sisters waged a terrible war against Cronus, who was helped by the Titans and Titanesses. Zeus was helped by Cronus's other brothers— the monsters who had been cast down to Tartarus and never set free. They fought with weapons of thunder, lightning, and earthquakes. Zeus was also helped by the kind and wise Prometheus, son of one of the Titans.

The war between Zeus and Cronus nearly ruined the universe. But Zeus eventually won, and a world that had been filled with fear became a world of beauty. The wounds on the earth that the war had caused soon healed, and the earth became green and fruitful again.

Now Zeus was lord of the universe. Unlike his father and grandfather, though, Zeus did not want to rule alone. He wanted to share his powers with his

A sculpture of Athena, goddess of wisdom, crafts, and war.

brothers and sisters, and later, some of his children. The one-eyed Cyclops built a huge palace for all the gods and goddesses on Mount Olympus, where they sat on golden thrones and reigned over heaven and earth.

Zeus, lord of the sky and father of the gods and people, sat on the highest throne. Hera, the queen, sat to his right. The other ten Olympians included Zeus's brothers and sisters, sons and daughters. They were: Poseidon, god of the sea and earthquakes; Hestia, goddess of the earth; Demeter, goddess of all growing things; Athena, goddess of wisdom, crafts, and war, and protector of the city of Athens; Aphrodite, goddess of love and beauty; Artemis, goddess of the moon and the hunt; Hermes, messenger to the gods, and protector of travelers and thieves; Ares, god of war; Apollo, the god of light, medicine, and poetry; and Hephaestus, the god of fire. Three other gods are also sometimes considered Olympians: Hades, god of the underworld; Dionysius, god of wine; and the hero Heracles.

The Greeks believed that all the gods and goddesses had special powers and would live forever. Yet they also believed that these beings looked like humans. Ancient Greeks believed the gods and goddesses had human feelings and faults. Zeus, for example, was known for his fits of temper, which could flare up without warning. When he was angry, he would hurl a thunderbolt through the heavens, causing lightning. The gods could also be warm and loving, such as Aphrodite, or kind and generous, such as Apollo, the friend of humans.

Demeter and Persephone

The story of Demeter and Persephone is an example of a myth that was created to explain something in nature. In this case, it explains how and why the seasons change.

Demeter, the powerful but loving mother of earth, often came down from Olympus to care for her crops.

Tall and dignified, with hair the color of ripe wheat, she could be seen striding through her fields with her daughter Persephone. Persephone was very sweet, and the valleys rang with the sound of her laughter.

Far down in the dark kingdom, Hades, god of the underworld, could hear Persephone's laughter. He longed to make her his wife.

One day, while running through a meadow, Persephone came upon a beautiful, sweet-smelling narcissus. She had never seen a flower so beautiful. As she reached out to pluck it, the earth opened up, and out leaped Hades. He grabbed the screaming Persephone, swept her into his chariot, and raced his coal-black stallions back to the underworld. Quickly, the earth closed over them.

Demeter had heard Persephone's cries, but she could not find her. She ran desperately around the meadow searching for her daughter. Demeter veiled herself in a black cloud and sped over the land and sea, asking everyone she met if they had seen her daughter. Apollo, who sees everything, told her that Hades had forced Persephone to become his wife, and Zeus had agreed to it.

Demeter wandered the earth, wasting away with longing for her daughter. Nothing grew on earth, and it became dry and lifeless. In her sorrow, Demeter had forgotten her duties as goddess of the harvest.

Zeus saw the dried, brown earth and became

Hermes, messenger of the gods.

worried. He sent the gods, one after another, to persuade Demeter to make the earth bear fruit again. "No," she answered. "Not until I have my daughter back."

Finally Zeus sent Hermes, messenger of the gods, down to Hades with an order to release Persephone. Hermes found Hades and Persephone sitting cold and silent on their thrones. He delivered Zeus's command, and Persephone jumped up in happiness. Hades became very sad because, in his own way, he loved Persephone. Yet he knew he must obey Zeus.

Hades suddenly had an idea. He took a pomegranate from a dish beside the throne and gave it to Persephone. In her hurry to get away from him, she quickly ate four of the fruit's seeds. She did not know, though, that the pomegranate was the food of the dead. Hades had tricked her into eating some, so she would have to return to him.

Persephone returned to earth, and mother and daughter cried out with joy as they hugged each other. Demeter, who had become a wrinkled, bent old woman in her grief, turned back into the stately, beautiful goddess.

Demeter blessed her fields. Flowers bloomed and grain ripened. All was light again until Persephone mentioned that she had eaten the food Hades had given her. Demeter knew the secret of the pomegranate, and she knew Persephone would have to return to Hades. But

Zeus took pity on Demeter and Persephone. He ruled that Persephone must return to Hades, but only for four months each year—one month for every seed she had eaten. Every year, when Persephone left for Hades, Demeter grew sad. The earth turned cold and nothing grew—this was winter. But when Persephone's footsteps could be heared as she rose from Hades, the whole earth burst into bloom. As long as mother and daughter were together, the earth was warm and bright.

The Kalikantzari

Not all of Greece's myths and legends come from ancient times. One favorite Christmas story was first told sometime during the Byzantine period. It is still told today and is part of the Christmas fun in many homes.

The Kalikantzari, a band of mischievous imps, live deep beneath the surface of the earth. Throughout the year, they are busy trying to destroy the large tree that holds up the earth. But for twelve days each year, from Christmas until the feast of the Epiphany (the baptism of Christ in the Greek Orthodox Church), the Kalikantzari come rushing up to the earth's surface, eager to work their pranks.

During these twelve days, all accidents are blamed on these troublemakers. They smash dishes, ring church bells, shake looms to make a weaver dizzy, and make people trip. They grow very large, then very small, then disappear altogether. They pounce on passersby and make them dance until they fall.

On the twelfth day, the people celebrate Epiphany. Priests sprinkle holy water everywhere to bring new life filled with goodness and hope. The Kalikantzari tremble from the holy water. They escape from the light of the upper world and race back to the bowels of the earth. While they were above the ground, the tree which holds up the earth grew back to its original size and thickness. Once again, the Kalikantzari begin chopping away at the tree, trying to shake the foundations of the earth.

Saints of Greece

After the Greeks adopted Christianity, some of their best-loved stories were about saints. Parents tell these stories to their children to teach them important values in life. They hope their children will be inspired by the saints' brave deeds and helpfulness to others.

Saint Stylianos was the patron saint of children. He was born in the seventeenth century to a very poor family, and from an early age, he devoted his life to Christ. When he grew up, he joined a group of hermits to live a life of thought and prayer. Unlike most hermits, he did not completely withdraw from society. In-

Paintings and sculptures honoring the saints of Greece can be found throughout the country.

stead, he went among people during the day and returned to his cave at night.

It is said that Saint Stylianos had the power to heal the sick. He devoted most of his time to helping either sick children or those needing guidance. Families from all social classes trusted Stylianos to teach their children. He was also famous for his big, beaming smile. According to legend, when he died, he had a smile on his face. Parents hope their children will be inspired by his story because he lived in service to others.

Greek parents also use proverbs to teach their children about what is important in life. When Greek parents wish to guide their children, they say such things as "Better to be alone than with bad company;" "Truth and sincerity are the basis of each virtue;" and "Learn to think of good and it will come."

Most Greeks love their myths, legends, folktales, and colorful sayings. Even now, with television and other entertainment, for many, nothing quite compares with a good conversation or a good story.

6. *Festivals and Feast Days*

The Greek calendar is filled with festivals. In villages, towns, and cities, one festival follows another nearly every day of the year. There are celebrations which show the powerful bond the Greeks feel with nature. Some celebrate the planting of the crops and the first harvest. Others celebrate the changing seasons, flowers, farm animals, and wildlife. In some villages in the Peloponnesus, boys parade down the street carrying painted carvings of swallows on poles, while singing traditional songs in honor of the swallows. This beautiful festival dates back to the time when the gods on Mount Olympus were worshiped.

Greece's link to the sea is also reflected in its festivals. Fishing celebrations are common on many islands and in coastal towns. Greece celebrates Navy Week with special entertainments. On the last day of this week, in the village of Aphisos, there is a ceremony to remember the Argonauts, heroes of Greek mythology. Propelled by oars and a sail, the *Argo 2* follows the same course which was, according to legend, taken by Jason and the Argonauts on the *Argo* in their search for the Golden Fleece.

Festivals celebrating the arts are very important in

The ancient Theater of Dionysius hosts classical drama festivals as well as modern concerts.

Greece, too. Each summer, people travel to sites such as Epidaurus and Philippi for classical drama festivals. Ancient theaters come alive again with the dramas and comedies of early Greek playwrights.

The Athens Festival is another important arts festival. Drama, both ancient and modern, and classical and rock music are performed at the Herod Atticus Theatre at the foot of the Acropolis. Many Greek artists, along with artists from all over the world, perform there.

There are a number of celebrations that honor local traditions. One of these takes place in the village of

Monoclissia. For a day, women and men trade their traditional roles. Every January 8, women leave the care of the children, the cooking, and the housework to their husbands. They walk through the streets and gather at the local cafe to drink and debate politics. If a man dares to leave his house before dusk, he becomes a prisoner of the women! At dusk, though, the men are invited to join the women in dining, singing, and dancing.

National Holidays

Greek Independence Day falls on March 25 and is celebrated throughout the country. Independence Day is the anniversary of the war of independence fought against the Turks. It is an exciting holiday for many Greeks. Children dress up in traditional national costumes, and parades and reenactments of important military events are held. Heroes such as Bouboulina, Kolokotronis, and the women of Souli are celebrated in short plays.

Labor Day, which falls on May 1, is another important national holiday. As in other countries throughout the world, Labor Day in Greece is a time to honor working people. Businesses and schools are closed, and labor groups hold rallies to celebrate. Many people visit the countryside to relax with their families and have picnics.

Saints' Days

In addition to nature, arts, and local traditions, the Greeks celebrate saints' days. According to the Greek Orthodox calendar, almost every day is sacred to some saint. Nearly every village, town, and city has a patron saint, and almost everyone in the community takes time to celebrate that saint's feast day. On the patron saint's special day, some priests dress in golden robes and lead parades through the streets of the village or town.

The feast of Saint Dionysius takes place each year on the island of Zaginthos in the Ionian Sea. The saint's glass coffin is paraded through the streets and passed over ill or physically disabled people. It is said that these people are often cured. It is widely believed that Saint Dionysius's spirit walks on the island, performing miracles.

The feast of Saint Constantine and his mother, Saint Helen, is celebrated throughout Greece. In some villages, Christian rites are mixed with some pre-Christian ones. In the traditional celebration, barefoot villagers dance around a bonfire holding pictures of Saint Constantine and Saint Helen. Then, people "possessed" by their spirits dance unharmed on live coals.

It is not only saints who are honored on their feast days. People with saints' names are honored, too. A saint's feast day is called a person's name day.

These women are taking part in a traditional saint's day celebration.

On a Greek's name day, the family might go to a church service and listen to a sermon about the saint being honored. Later, the priest gives all those bearing the saint's name a piece of special holy bread and a blessing. Throughout the day, friends and relatives drop by, bringing toys, books, or clothing. They also bring wishes of *"Chronia polla"* ("Many years"), and hug and kiss the special person named after the saint. Some parents may decide to give their child a special name-day party. In that case, a dinner would be served, including the child's favorite foods and pastries.

Name days are special occasions in Greece. They are just one of the many traditions that add beauty and warmth to people's lives, and strengthen the bonds between them.

Easter Traditions

Of all the religious holidays in Greece, Easter is the most important. The Easter season lasts for many weeks, and each part of it has special customs.

A month of Carnival is celebrated throughout Greece before Lent, the forty weekdays before Easter. Carnival is the time for music and laughter, for practical jokes, dressing up in colorful costumes, feasting, and dancing in the streets. The city of Patras is especially well known for its Carnival. The people have a parade with marching bands, floats, giant figures, and clowns. Delicious chocolates wrapped in foil are tossed from the floats into the waiting crowds. Children leap into the air in an attempt to catch as many chocolates as they can.

The first day of Lent is called Clean Monday. Lenten lunches are packed and families may go off to the country for picnics. Children usually bring a kite with them, and then try to see who can fly his or her kite the highest.

The Lenten period lasts for seven weeks. The rules of the Greek Orthodox Church on fasting during Lent are very strict. It is forbidden to eat meat, eggs, fish, or milk products on Wednesdays and Fridays, and during Holy Week, which is the week before Easter.

A few days before Easter, it is common for many city people to leave their homes for villages. Sometimes these villages are where they were born, or they may simply be where the family has a country house. In either case, celebrating Easter in a small village church is a big part of the Easter tradition for many Greeks.

On Holy Thursday, Greek families get together and boil eggs, much as American families do. However, most eggs are then dyed red, to remind people of the blood of Christ. The eggs are then polished with olive oil until they shine. Eggs are supposed to be dyed only on Holy Thursday and Holy Saturday. Any other day, especially Holy Friday, is considered bad luck.

On Holy Friday, the *tsoureki*, or Easter bread, is baked. Tsoureki is a sweet, braided bread with a shiny glaze. It is topped with the red-dyed eggs. The tsoureki dough is often shaped into little baskets, animal shapes, or tiny loaves topped with just one egg for children. Holy Friday, or Good Friday as it is also called, is the only day Easter bread may be baked.

On the evening of Holy Saturday, many Greeks go to church carrying an unlighted candle. Just before midnight, the lights in the church are put out, and everyone stands in the darkness. This is a symbol of the darkness

Villagers parade through the streets as a part of their Easter celebration.

of the world without Christ. Then, the priest appears from behind an altar screen carrying a lighted candle. One person lights his or her candle from the priest's candle. One by one, each member of the congregation lights the candle of his or her neighbor, until hundreds of flames glow in the darkness. After the service, the churchgoers make their way home, sheltering the lighted candles. A lighted candle is believed to bring blessings into the home. The strict fast of the last week of Lent is ended by a late meal that includes Easter bread, cheese, and *mayeritsa*, an egg and lemon soup with lamb.

On Easter Sunday, roast lamb is the main dish at mealtime. After dinner, children and parents take part in the tradition of egg cracking. First, the mother or father selects a dyed egg, then turns to the person on the right, who is also holding an egg. The parent tries to crack the second person's egg with his or her own. The eggs are held lightly in the hand so that only the tips show. If the first person successfully cracks the other's egg, he or she may continue down the table until his or her egg is cracked. That is the sign for the rest of the family to join in, and soon everyone is trying to crack each other's egg.

Christmas in Greece

Christmas is another important Greek holiday. Like Easter, it has many interesting traditions. Greek children have several Christmas customs of their own. For example, two days before Christmas, children in some villages join together to drag bundles of firewood to the village square. After dark, they light bonfires and sing and dance.

On Christmas Eve, children from the country and city usually run from house to house singing *kalanda*

(Christmas carols), while clanging small metal triangles and beating clay drums. Along with religious themes, kalanda include good wishes and praise to members of each family. Carolers are often offered chestnuts or walnuts, and sometimes even Christmas buns.

Early on Christmas morning, many Greek families go to church. Children dress in their finest clothes. After church, families rush home to make last-minute preparations for Christmas dinner. The first item to go on the table is the *christopsomo*, or Christ bread. The Christopsomo is a large, colorful, sweet loaf of bread in various shapes. Decorations, which are cut into the bread's crust, usually have something to do with the family's life or professions. For example, a farming family's christopsomo might be decorated with a plow and oxen.

After the Christ bread is laid out, it is surrounded by a pot of honey and dried fruit, almonds, and walnuts. Then, the father usually makes the sign of the cross over the loaf of bread with his knife, and wishes everyone "Chronia polla!" He cuts the loaf and gives everyone a slice. Several other dishes may follow. These may vary from place to place, but pork is almost always the main dish. In many villages, the pig has been fattened for months before Christmas.

After Christmas dinner, some people pour wine over their hearths. This custom dates back to the time when the goddess of the hearth, Hestia, was honored in this way. Most Greek families do not exchange gifts on Christmas. Presents are usually given on Saint Basil's Day, which falls on New Year's Day.

At midnight on New Year's Eve, Greek families share a *vasilopeta* (Saint Basil's cake). A coin, usually a gold one, is baked inside. It is believed that the person who gets the piece with the coin will be lucky all year.

Greece has many exciting festivals and holidays. Each one tells us a great deal about its people, as well as the traditions they cherish and hold onto in the modern world.

7. *Hospitality, Family, and Food*

To most Greeks, family is the most important thing in the world. Parents, children, grandparents, aunts, uncles, cousins, godparents, and even close friends are all considered to be family. Members of a Greek family feel a deep loyalty and sense of responsibility toward each other. When most Greeks have a problem, they can count on their family for support and advice.

Greek families are usually very open about expressing emotions. They also take great pride in each other's accomplishments, and enjoy sharing these feelings of pride with others. In fact, there is an old Greek proverb which says, "If you don't sing the praises of your house, it will fall down on you."

Greek homes are usually lively places. Friends and relatives may drop in often for informal gatherings. Because most elderly people live with their grown children and grandchildren, a Greek house may seem crowded to some Americans. Grandparents in Greece are honored by their families, and children are taught to respect them from a very young age. A Greek child may spend a lot of time with his or her grandparents, listening to stories, getting advice, and learning different skills. This respect for elders is a part of the Greek philotemo.

Greek children usually spend a great deal of time with their grandparents.

In the past, the father made most of the important decisions about the family. In modern Greece, however, this is changing. Many young people feel that marriage should be an equal partnership, where men and women share in decision-making and chores. Still, many men do not help with the housework or cooking, even if the mother works outside the home.

Raising the children, however, has always been a shared responsibility. Greek fathers are known for being very strict. This does not mean, though, that Greek fathers are responsible only for discipline. Most men try to involve themselves in their children's activities, such as homework and sports. Greek fathers are also usually affectionate toward their children.

Mothers, too, are treated with great respect in Greece. Traditionally, a mother was admired because of her devotion to her family and her dedication to providing a loving home. Even today, while many women have careers outside their home, almost all put their families first. In Greece, mothers are honored in poems, folk songs, and proverbs.

Beloved Children

The birth of a child is considered to be a very important moment in the life of a Greek couple. Sometimes parents and grandparents are moved to write songs or poems about the newborn baby.

Children are usually at the center of their parents' lives. Many are raised to feel that they are special and important people. They are raised to be responsible, too. Girls are expected to help with the cooking and the housework, and boys usually do any chores outside the house. Often, the sons of fishermen will help their fathers mend nets, or fish. Both sons and daughters of farming families help with the farming and feed the livestock, while the children of merchants might help around the store.

Greek children are expected to devote much of their time to their families. From an early age, Greek children take part in family gatherings, such as baptisms, weddings, name days, and other celebrations. In this way, they learn to behave well with people of all ages. Children are expected to be kind and polite to their elders, too.

In addition to special celebrations, families share many activities together. They might go to the movies or theater with each other, or take an evening stroll. In the past, this togetherness was common even when children got married. After marriage, couples usually lived with the husband's family. Today, however, this is beginning to change. Fewer young people are choosing to stay at home. Instead, they buy homes of their own as soon as they can.

At one time, marriages were arranged by parents, and it was a young person's duty to marry whomever his or her parents had chosen. Most matches were made for practical reasons, such as money. Sometimes, women had no say about whom they married. One elderly woman from Corinth, remembering her wedding day, said, "How I longed to run away! But I could not disgrace my parents." She added, however, "I was lucky. My husband and I grew to love each other."

Today, few marriages are arranged. Most young people are now allowed to date, and the decision about whom to marry is left up to them—with some parental advice, of course!

Homes and Food

Most middle-class homes in Greece are small and simply furnished, compared to some American houses. Wealthy people might live in large homes and beautiful villas, while poorer Greeks might live in apartment buildings or tiny, run-down houses. Yet large or small, rich or poor, these homes have one thing in common—a garden. During the warm months, courtyards and gardens are bursting with flowers. Blossoms tumble over balconies everywhere, creating floating gardens in the air.

Many people have vegetable as well as flower gardens, which are lovingly tended. Gardens might have grapevines, fruit trees, vegetables, and towering geranium and rose plants. It is common for families to eat most of their meals in the garden if the weather is good.

Greeks eat mostly simple, healthy foods. *Fassolatha*, a bean soup, is a common dish which is very simple to make. It is cooked at least once a week in Greek villages, and is eaten hot in the winter and cold in the summer. Fassolatha is usually served with fresh bread, some olives, tomatoes, and cheese.

Salads are also very popular among Greeks. They accompany almost any meal, unless boiled greens such

Flowers decorate even the smallest balconies in Greece.

as dandelion leaves or wild chicory are served. Salads usually contain tomatoes, cucumbers, black olives, onions or scallions, lettuce, green peppers, and *feta* cheese. Feta is the best known of the many Greek cheeses. It is a slightly tangy white cheese made from the milk of goats. *Kasseri*, a mild and buttery cheese, is almost as popular as feta cheese in Greece.

To the Greeks living along the coast or on islands, seafood is an everyday dish. The Ionian, Aegean, and Mediterranean seas offer a great variety of fish and sea-food—red snapper, sardines, halibut, octopus, squid, and shrimp, to name a few.

Lamb is the most popular meat in Greece. Chicken, pork, and beef are enjoyed, too. Meats are often grilled over hot coals on outdoor spits, but are also eaten in stews, or ground up to include in casseroles.

Fresh fruits and vegetables are an important part of every Greek's diet. Many people who live in towns and cities like to buy them weekly at the *liekey*, an open-air market. Here, they can find all types of produce grown in Greece, as well as meats and cheeses.

Most Greeks are very fond of sweets. In Greece, sweets are not just eaten after meals. They are eaten anytime, from morning until night. Parents take their children to *zacharoplasteions*, or sweet shops, in the early evening to peer through the window and choose their own dessert. Among the favorites are *baklava*, thin

A Greek man shops at a liekey*, an open-air market, in Athens.*

layers of dough baked and topped with nuts and honey, and *galatoboureko*, a fluffy milk and honey custard floating on sheets of dough.

Mealtimes

Most Greeks have a light breakfast. They might eat boiled eggs and toast, hot milk and honey, or yoghurt with fruit and *paximathi*, a plain biscuit.

Breakfasts are light because lunch is the main meal of the day. At about one thirty in the afternoon, family members return from school or work to share the meal with their families. Some typical main courses are chicken with yoghurt sauce, *dolmathes* (stuffed vine leaves covered with egg and lemon sauce), *souvlaki* (lamb grilled on a spit), *moussaka* (minced meat and eggplant), and *pastitsio* (baked macaroni and meat).

It is customary in Greece for people to take naps after they finish eating. Working people usually don't return to their jobs until 5:00 P.M. and often work until 8:00 P.M. Many people nap so that they will have the strength to stay up late at night. Then they visit with friends and family or go to *tavernas* and *bouzoukia*, and are still able to get up for work the next morning!

Greek families usually eat a light dinner around nine o'clock at night. They often have just a small piece of broiled meat, a salad, or perhaps a feta cheese omelette. Children stay up much later in Greece than they do in the United States or Canada. They, too, take naps in the afternoon. They usually go out with their parents late in the evening. On weekends, when parents are out having a late dinner or sweets in restaurants, children can be found riding their bicycles in nearby parks past midnight!

Here are a few Greek recipes to try. Your friends and family are sure to enjoy them. And when everyone is seated around the table, don't forget to wish your guests, *"Kali orexi"* ("Good appetite")!

Tzatziki
(Cucumber and Yoghurt Dip)

1 medium cucumber, peeled
1 clove crushed garlic, or 1 teaspoon garlic powder
3 scallions (or green onions), finely chopped
1 teaspoon olive oil
1/2 teaspoon white vinegar
1 teaspoon finely chopped dill
1 cup plain yoghurt

Cut the cucumber in half lengthwise and scoop out seeds. Cut the cucumber into tiny chunks. In a small bowl, mix the cucumber with the garlic, scallions, olive oil, vinegar, and dill. Add the yoghurt, and stir gently to combine. Cover and chill for two hours or more. Serve tzatziki as a dip with crackers or raw vegetables. Makes about one cup.

The following recipe is the classic Greek salad featuring feta cheese. Feta can be bought in most cheese stores and many supermarkets.

Greek Salad

1/2 head iceburg or romaine lettuce
2 quartered tomatoes
1/2 green pepper, cored, seeded, and sliced into strips
5 scallions (or green onions), thinly sliced
1 cucumber, peeled and sliced
1 cup (about 6 ounces) feta cheese, broken into chunks
12 to 16 black Greek olives

Combine all of the above ingredients in a large salad bowl and serve. Greek salad can be eaten plain or with your favorite dressing. Serves 4.

This popular Greek entree is easy to make!

Baked Chicken Oregano

6 whole chicken breasts
1/2 cup olive oil
1/2 cup lemon juice
1/4 cup dried oregano leaves
2 teaspoons dried thyme leaves
1 teaspoon salt
1/2 teaspoon pepper

Turn your oven on to its highest setting—broil.

Rinse the chicken. Pat dry. Arrange the chicken in a deep, rectangular baking pan. Place the olive oil, lemon juice, oregano, thyme, salt, and pepper in a jar with a tight-fitting lid. Cover and shake.

Pour one-third of this mixture over the chicken. Broil this until the chicken becomes golden brown on top. Now turn the chicken over on its other side. Pour one-third of the olive oil mixture over it and broil until this side, too, is golden brown. Turn the oven temperature down to 350°. Add 1/2 cup water and bake chicken for one hour. While the chicken is baking, brush the remaining olive oil mixture over the top from time to time. Serves 6.

8. *School Days*

School is an important part of a Greek child's life, just as it is for many children throughout the world. Most Greek young people take their schoolwork seriously. From the time they are little, they are taught that having a good education is one of the greatest treasures anyone can have.

Greek students have a lot in common with students from the United States and Canada. They attend school five days a week, from Monday through Friday. They study history, geography, reading, and math, just as North Americans do. Recess, vacations, and field trips are a part of their lives, too. A Greek student also has to think about homework and getting good grades. Yet in other ways, being a student in Greece is quite different from being a student in North America.

Greek children do not attend school for as many hours as North Americans. First and second graders go to school for only four and a half hours each day. From third grade through sixth grade, students attend school for five hours a day—usually from eight o'clock in the morning until one o'clock in the afternoon. Another difference is that religion is studied in all Greek schools, from third grade through senior high.

Two young friends do their homework together after school.

Elementary School

Greek elementary school begins with the first grade and goes through the sixth. Children have the same teacher all day, but they do not have the same schedule each day. Some subjects, such as the Greek language and math, are taught every day. Other subjects, though, such as history or geography, are taught only three times a week. Art, music, and physical education classes are usually held only once a week.

Letters are given for grades in Greek elementary

schools. An *A* stands for excellent work, *B* for good, and *C* means average and below average. No one gets a failing grade in elementary school—it is the policy to promote everyone. Still, many students do not like getting *C*s, and set higher standards for themselves.

In the first and second grades, students concentrate on arithmetic and learning how to read and write Greek. From the third grade on, their schedules include history, geography, physics, chemistry, arithmetic, geometry, religion, art, and music. Grade school students have between one and two hours of homework each day. With their short school day, they have a lot of free time to play!

Greek young people look forward to school field trips. They might visit the ancient temples of gods and goddesses, beautiful old Byzantine churches, museums, farms, or manufacturing plants. A class might take a boat ride to a neighboring island and spend the day at the beach, or explore one of the many caves in Greece.

Junior and Senior High

Greek students attend *gymnasio*, which are like American junior high schools, between the seventh and ninth grades. In seventh grade, students begin having different teachers for different subjects. They also begin studying many subjects—eighteen, to be exact! Some

Schoolchildren on a field trip to the National Gardens.

subjects, such as modern Greek, math, and religion, are studied throughout the year. But others, such as physics, chemistry, and anthropology, are only studied part of the year. Since most subjects are taken only a few hours a week, a gymnasium student's life is not quite as hard as it first sounds.

The Greek school year is divided into three periods of three months each. At the end of each period, all pupils are given oral and written tests. In order to be promoted to the next grade, students must get passing grades in each subject for each of the three-month periods. In gymnasio, numbers are given for grades instead of letters. Pupils must get a mark of at least ten in each subject to pass, with the highest grade being twenty. Gymnasio students, unlike elementary school students, have a lot of homework and little free time.

When students graduate from gymnasio, they are faced with several choices. They can go to work, or they can continue their education at the two main kinds of senior high schools—the technical and vocational *lykeion*, and the general lykeion.

Technical and vocational lykeions teach subjects such as electronics, printing, plumbing, road building, jewelry making, and office work. The purpose of these lykeions is to prepare students to get a job once they graduate. Special examinations must be passed before students are awarded certificates in technical and vocational lykeions. This is also true of general lykeions.

General lykeions prepare students for university study. In general lykeions, history, literature, and ancient Greek, as well as other subjects, are studied. Pupils all take the same courses the first two years. During the last year, they choose the major, or main subject, they hope to study at a university. They concentrate very hard on this special subject, taking many hours of classes in it each week. Then, at the end of the school year, they

A gymnasio *classroom.*

take an exam in their major in order to be accepted at a university.

There have been many changes in the Greek school system in recent years. For example, there is much less rote learning, or memorizing, than there was in the past. In the higher grades, teachers now encourage students to think for themselves rather than simply teaching the facts. Even in the lower grades, children are encouraged to speak up and even disagree with their teachers. They are also expected to be polite, and to back up their opinions with facts.

This educational philosophy can be seen in a tenth-grade physics class near Athens. As the teacher writes a theory on the board, the class copies it down in their notebooks. One of the students, a girl named Sophia, becomes upset. She tells her teacher that the theory does not make sense to her, given her knowledge of physics. She then states her reasons for suspecting that the theory is false. A short and lively discussion follows between Sophia and her teacher. The teacher is very proud of his student, even though they were not able to settle the matter. This type of participation is encouraged in Greek classrooms.

Instructors also try to teach their students values. A plaque hangs on the wall in the hallway of a Spartan school. It reads, "Religion, Country, Family, Kindness, Give the Best of Yourself to Others." Stavros, a ten-year-old in fifth grade at the school, reads these words each time he enters his classroom.

Stavros says he enjoys going to school most of the time. He admits, though, that there are times he would much rather be playing soccer with his friends or watching television. But Stavros dreams of becoming a doctor some day, so he knows he has to study hard to reach his goal.

Stavros likes reading poems and stories from all

over the world in his literature book. For homework, he might have to read a poem by George Seferis, or learn about Thor Heyerdahl's adventures in *Kon Tiki.*

Stavros has a cousin named Andreas who lives in a village outside of Sparta. Andreas is preparing to take an exam in mathematics soon in order to get into a university. He knows there are many more applicants than places available at the university. Only the students who get the highest scores are accepted. Andreas has been studying for weeks. He has given up going out with friends, watching television, and even reading for pleasure. Yet these seem like small sacrifices to him.

Like so many Greeks, Andreas is willing to work very hard to get a good education. In fact, a university education is so valued in Greece that some parents hire tutors for their children as soon as they enter the first grade. To many Greeks, education will help guarantee them and their country a bright future.

9. Sports and Fun

The Greeks have always valued sports and physical fitness. The ancient Greeks believed that training the body was just as important as training the mind. An athlete was considered a special person, singled out by the gods for his grace and power. Many modern Greeks share this feeling.

Although the Olympic Games began in Greece in 776 B.C., they were no longer held after A.D. 394, when Greece was under Byzantine and Turkish rule. In 1896, however, the Olympics were reborn. The first modern games were held in Athens. A new stadium was built over an ancient stadium for the first celebration. More than 280 athletes from 13 nations competed, and Greece's Spyros Louis won a gold medal for the marathon. Since then, the Olympics have been very important to many Greeks. Several Greek athletes have won medals and other honors for their skills. Since 1980, Greek men have won three medals in Greco-Roman wrestling, and one in yachting.

Greek women have become champions, too. Sophia Sacorafa broke the women's world record for the javelin in 1984. Anna Verouli became the javelin-throwing champion in the European Games in the same year. She became a national hero. Since then, many young girls have been inspired to take part in javelin throwing. Running, jumping, and other field events are also popular among young girls.

A special program called Child in Sports has been supported by the Greek government. The purpose of this program is to discover and develop talented young athletes. Afterschool training centers have been set up in some public gyms. Boys and girls are trained in their favorite sports, such as swimming, soccer, volleyball, basketball, and handball.

Volleyball and basketball are the most popular girls' sports, while most boys prefer to play soccer. Throughout the country, boys like to kick around a soccer ball—in school yards, country roads, and city streets. Many Greek boys dream of becoming soccer players when they grow up. Great soccer players are national heroes. A comic book, *Eric Castel*, tells about the adventures of a fictional soccer hero. It is read by boys all over Greece.

Soccer is the most popular team sport in Greece. There are more than seventy professional and semiprofessional teams, and hundreds of non-professional teams throughout the country. Professional matches are played on Saturdays and Sundays from September to June. These games are often on television.

Professional soccer teams also play teams from

other countries. The national team of Greece is Ethniki Omada. When there is an important game, such as the European Cup Championship or World Cup Championship, there are few Greeks on the streets—they are either at the stadium or watching the match on television.

Traditional Fun

Swimming is one of the best-loved sports in Greece. For many people, the sea is a constant source of relaxation and fun. Many Greeks live close enough to the sea to go swimming every day. Most swim between April and October, when the weather is warm, but some swim year-round. There are hundreds of beaches in Greece, and some are considered among the best in the world. The seas are usually calm, and crystal clear in many places.

After swimming, Greek children might build sand castles, collect seashells, or run along the shore flying their kites. Families often pack picnic lunches or dinners and bring them to the beach.

There are many clubs throughout Greece for children who like to swim. There are also surfing, wind surfing, and skin diving clubs for boys and girls interested in these sports. Water sports are popular with adults, too, especially sailing, skin diving, wind surfing, and water polo.

Swimming and other water sports are very popular with Greeks of all ages.

Greek children enjoy many of the same activities as children from North America. Boys and girls play chess, checkers, and board games. Some children enjoy building models of planes, cars, and ships. Girls, especially, might collect dolls in regional costumes, or play hopscotch, jump rope, and sing rhyming songs that go along with the skipping games.

This is a translation of a popular playground rhyme:

Where are you going, Miss Maria, Miss Maria?
You can't pass, you can't pass!

I am going to the garden, to the garden, to the garden.
What do you there in the garden?
I am going to pick some violets.
What shall you do with the violets, Miss Maria, Miss Maria?
I shall give them to my dearest friend!

Besides playing games, Greek children like going to amusement parks and movies, as well as watching television. Since the late 1970s, American video games have become very popular—Pacman and Karate Champ are great favorites. Many young people read American comic books, too, which are translated into Greek. These include *Tom and Jerry* and *Spider Man.*

Traditional Greek entertainment is popular, too. One favorite is attending the Karagiozi Theatre. This shadow-puppet theater stars a penniless wanderer called Karagiozi. Children love to watch his silly adventures. The Karagiozi Theatre is always a noisy place—children can't help shouting warnings to their little hero.

Family Trips

Many Greeks, whether children or adults, like taking family trips to lakes, the seashore, national parks, and other places of natural beauty. Often, families just

The Karagiozi Theatre.

go for a day-long outing, but sometimes they bring their camping equipment and stay for several days. Some of the national parks in Greece have wild goats, waterfowl, rabbits, wolves, and foxes living in them.

In Athens, Zapion Park and the National Gardens are very popular with families. Variety shows, featuring singers, dancers, jugglers, and acrobats, are often performed there. Vendors sell ices and sodas for the thirsty visitors.

The National Gardens are filled with a great number and variety of plants and trees. Visitors can feed the ducks, geese, and swans by the lake. They can also watch peacocks and turtles wander freely through the thickets. The National Gardens can be a peaceful break from the crowded city of Athens.

Going on day or weekend trips to caves is very popular in Greece, too. The Dirou Cave in southern Greece is a well-known underground cave with a river flowing through it. People explore the cave by riding in rowboats along winding waterways which are filled with beautiful stalactites and stalagmites.

Another favorite kind of short trip is a visit to a site where a Greek myth is said to have taken place. Families can take a trip to the cave in Crete that is the mythical birthplace of Zeus. They can also tour the island of Seriphos, where twisted cliffs along the shore resemble human figures. According to legend, these cliffs were people turned to stone by Medusa, a monster who had snakes for hair.

Visiting mountain resorts is another popular vacation. Pilion, outside Volos in northern Greece, and Metsovo, also in the north, are well-known resorts. At these resorts, children can go hiking, swimming, boating, and take part in a variety of other sports.

The most popular vacation of all—for both Greeks and tourists—is exploring the many Greek islands.

A guide sits among the stalactites and stalagmites in Dirou Cave.

Whether they have visited an island once, or have been there many times before, people find that each island is different and has much to offer. To many Greeks, exploring their own country is always an adventure. They are proud of Greece, and feel it would take an entire lifetime to really know all of it. Many Greeks are also proud to have monasteries, palaces, churches, temples, and pirate lairs in their own hometown. These are just some of the things that make it exciting to live in Greece.

10. A New Odyssey

The Greeks have always been a nation of emigrants. Since ancient times, they have sailed away to strange lands in search of new homes and adventure.

Many of the people who left Greece were poor farmers who had been unable to earn a living from the stony land. As hard as their lives had been, many were still sad to sail away from their homeland. Wherever they settled, they kept the same kind of government they had in their city-state, held onto their language and traditions, and built temples to their gods and goddesses.

The Greeks have settled all over the world. It is said that the first Greek to explore the United States was a sailor named Theodore. He sailed with a Spanish ship to Florida in 1637. One of the first Greek settlements in the New World was the colony of New Smyrna in Florida, established in 1767. Greeks came in search of gold during the California gold rush, and Greek merchants and sailors fought during the American Civil War.

Greek Pioneers

Before 1890, there were only about 3,000 Greeks living in the United States. Mass Greek immigration to the United States began in the 1890s and ended in the 1920s. About 450,000 Greeks entered the United States during this period.

These people began leaving Greece because of terrible poverty. At that time, the Greek economy depended on the export of currants (small raisins). When the crop failed due to a drought, the economy collapsed.

America became the promised land for Greeks. Steamship agents amazed *kafenion* (coffeehouse) audiences with stories about making fortunes in America. Labor agents from the United States in search of cheap labor came to the villages with promises of jobs. The Greek government encouraged emigration, too. It knew that the emigrants would probably send money back to Greece to help support their families. The emigrants might also return with money to invest in Greek industry. These funds helped Greece financially.

In the 1890s, family clans gathered to decide which one of their male members would go. They pooled their money and gave it to him. It was expected that he, in turn, would send money for the boat trip to brothers, uncles, and male cousins.

Emigrants were usually young or middle-aged. Some were married with children. Few women went with their husbands because money was so scarce. Many couples were separated for years, and some children did not remember their fathers.

Troubles in America

Most of the emigrants were shepherds and farmers who had rarely been away from their villages before. The great size of America was a shock to many. Yet their religion, their philotemo, and their pride in their heritage gave them strength for the difficult times that faced them.

Some Greeks headed for the western states to work on railroad gangs or in mines. Others went to New England mill towns to work in textile factories. Greeks who went to large northern cities such as New York and Chicago worked in factories, or as dishwashers, food or flower peddlers, or shoeshine boys. They worked long hours and sometimes slept as many as ten in a room in the cheapest apartments they could find. Some who could not find work right away were greeted with abuse and violence. They were often arrested and jailed because they did not know any English, did not have jobs, and did not have a place to live.

Those who did find work were often seen as a threat to the older, more established immigrant groups. Many Greeks were willing to work for lower wages than some other groups. Sometimes they were disliked simply because they looked and acted differently.

Like the immigrants before them, the Greek immigrants tried to make up for their uprooted lives by forming close-knit neighborhoods, ethnic societies, and churches. Often, the first thing the Greek immigrants did was to build a neighborhood church, which became the heart of the community. They also built kafenions and, later, restaurants and shops.

As close-knit as the Greek communities were, many people still felt homesick. At gatherings, they would toast each other, saying "*Seeyion kali patritha!*" ("To your health and to our homeland!") Many early Greek immigrants wanted to return home as quickly as possible. Forty percent of the people who left Greece between 1890 and 1920 did just that. The ones who came back wealthy built schools and churches in their native villages and had streets named after them!

Greek Americans

Many of those who remained in the United States sent for their wives and children, or for picture brides—marriages arranged by their families from across the ocean. Just as in their homeland, the majority of Greek women did not work outside their homes. Some, though, worked in textile or shoe factories, or in family stores.

Nearly every immigrant community had a Greek language newspaper. In 1911, the Greeks published more newspapers in relation to their numbers than any

Greek immigrants at a picnic in New York City in the 1920s.

other ethnic group. These newspapers were devoted to preserving Greek language, traditions, and culture. They also carried world news and news from Greece.

In 1920, many Greeks already owned small businesses. Flower peddlers bought flower shops, and bootblacks became owners of shoe repair shops. Waiters, dishwashers, and fruit and food peddlers became owners of restaurants and ice cream parlors. The first soda fountain was established in a Greek ice cream parlor, and the first sundae was said to have been invented by Greeks living in Chicago.

The American Hellenic Educational Progressive Association (AHEPA) was organized in 1922. Its president stated in 1925, "Today, 90 percent of our compatriots [fellow Greeks] have definitely decided to remain in America. This is the country where they will die, the country where their children will live." AHEPA became the leading Greek-American organization. Today, it stresses American (and Greek) history. It also encourages Greeks to take part in American society.

Greek immigration fell when strict quotas went into effect in the 1920s. From 1930 to 1950, an average of nine hundred Greek immigrants came to the United States each year. When quotas were lifted in the early 1960s, immigration rose again.

Some of the new immigrants had been village dwellers with little education. Many ended up running successful businesses, just like the immigrants in the past. But new kinds of immigrants came, too—medical school graduates, engineers, and other professionals. They came to the United States in search of better opportunities than they would have had in Greece. Like the early Greek immigrants and their families, they have kept strong ties to their homeland.

Greek-American children usually attend Greek language schools. They may also go to Sunday School to study the Greek Orthodox faith. Many join Greek Orthodox Youth of America (GOYA). Almost every Greek

Orthodox parish has a GOYA chapter where teenagers learn about religion and culture. They also get involved in social programs and athletics, and hold drives to help the needy in the United States and other countries.

Celebrating holiday feast days also helps Greek-American children remember their heritage. They look forward to cracking Easter eggs after Easter dinner, or to the vasilopeta being sliced on New Year's Day. In coastal cities and towns, many Greek Americans celebrate Epiphany with the blessing of the waters.

In addition to GOYA, there are countless organizations in the United States that promote Greek heritage. The Hellenic Cultural Circle organizes festivals, folk dancing groups, and lectures about Greek traditions and culture. The Society of the Preservation of Greek Heritage sponsors lectures about Greek subjects. The Metropolitan Greek Chorale sings, among other things, the works of Greek poets such as Elytis. *Pegasus* is an educational children's magazine written in both Greek and English. It explores Greek history, religion, mythology, and traditions. And in Astoria, New York, one can even visit a Karagiozi Theatre.

Many Accomplishments

Greek Americans and their children have interests that go beyond preserving the traditions of their home-

A young Greek American dressed in traditional clothing takes part in a Greek Independence Day celebration.

land. They love America, too, and are eager to make contributions to American culture. Many Greek Americans have become famous for their accomplishments.

Maria Anna Cecilia Sofia Kalogeropoulos, better known as Maria Callas, was a great opera star. The daughter of an immigrant, she grew up in a tough neighborhood of New York that was once called Hell's Kitchen. Maria Callas had a long, exciting career, and was well known and admired all over the world. At the peak of her career, her voice was able to cover nearly three octaves, something few singers can do.

Greek Americans have done well in politics, too. Michael Dukakis was the governor of Massachusetts for three terms. In 1988, he was the Democratic party's candidate for president of the United States. Although he lost the election, his campaign received a great deal of support from the Greek-American community.

There have also been many successful Greek-American businesspeople. Tom Carvel is probably one of the best known. He began selling ice cream in 1934 when he borrowed fifteen dollars from his future wife and filled his old vending truck with ice cream. Today, the 78-year-old Carvel has ice cream stores in eighteen states and a half dozen countries. He even runs a training course called the "Carvel College of Ice Cream Knowledge" for people who want to manage his stores.

The story of Greek immigrants in America is still unfolding. Every year, new immigrants arrive, seeking opportunities they cannot find in Greece. Many come to love their adopted country. Yet they never forget their Greek traditions, and they never forget their homeland, which holds a sacred place in their hearts.

Appendix A

Greek Embassies and Consulates in the United States and Canada

The Greek consulates in the United States and Canada offer assistance and information about all aspects of Greek life. For more information and resource materials, contact the embassy or consulate nearest you.

U.S. Consulates and Embassy

Atlanta, Georgia
Consulate of Greece
Tower Place, Suite 1670
3440 Peachtree Road, N.E.
Atlanta, Georgia 30026
Phone (404) 261-3313

Boston, Massachusetts
Consulate of Greece
Statler Office Building
20 Park Place
Boston, Massachusetts 02116
Phone (617) 542-3240

Chicago, Illinois
Consulate General of Greece
168 North Michigan Avenue
Chicago, Illinois 60601
Phone (312) 372-5355

New Orleans, Louisiana
Consulate of Greece
2318 Int'l. Trade Mart Bldg.

New Orleans, Louisiana 70130
Phone (504) 523-1167

New York, New York
Consulate General of Greece
69 East 79th Street
New York, New York 10021
Phone (212) 988-5500

San Francisco, California
Consulate General of Greece
2441 Gough Street
San Francisco, California 94123
Phone (415) 775-2102

Washington, D.C.
Embassy of Greece
2221 Massachusetts Avenue, N.W.
Washington, D.C. 20036
Phone (202) 645-7100

Canadian Consulates and Embassy

Montreal, Quebec
Greek Consulate General
2000 Peel Street, Suite 925
Montreal, Quebec H3A 2W5
Phone (514) 845-2105

Ottawa, Ontario
Embassy of Greece
80 McLaren Street
Ottawa, Ontario K2P 0K6
Phone (613) 238-6271

Toronto, Ontario
Greek Consulate General
100 University Street, Suite 1004
Toronto, Ontario M5G 1V6
Phone (416) 593-1636

Vancouver, British Columbia
Greek Consulate
1200 Burrard Street
Vancouver, British Columbia
  V6Z 2C7
Phone (604) 681-1381

Appendix B

Pronunciation Guide for Greek Names and Places

The following is a list of pronunciations to some Greek names, including people in ancient Greece, and the names of Greek towns and geographic features. All other pronunciations appear in the glossary, which follows this appendix.

People of Ancient Greece

Agamemnon (ag-uh-MEHM-nahn)

Aphrodite (af-ruh-DY-tee)

Apollo (uh-PAHL-oh)

Archimedes (ahr-kuh-MEED-eez)

Ares (AYR-eez)

Aristotle (AR-uh-staht-uhl)

Cleisthenes (klys-thuh-NEEZ)

Demeter (dih-MEET-uhr)

Dionysius (dy-uh-NIHS-ee-uhs)

Eristratos (eh-REE-strah-tohs)

Euripedes (yu-RIHP-uh-deez)

Gaea (JEE-uh)

Hades (HAY-deez)

Hera (HEER-uh)

Heracles (HEHR-uh-kleez)

Hermes (HUHR-meez)

Hestia (HEHS-tee-uh)

Medusa (mih-DOO-suh)

Menelaus (MEHN-uhl-ay-uhs)

Pericles (PEHR-uh-klees)

Persephone (puhr-SEHF-uh-nee)

Poseidon (puh-SYD-uhn)

Prometheus (prah-MEE-thee-uhs)

Rhea (REE-uh)

Socrates (SAHK-ruh-teez)

Sophocles (SAHF-uh-kleez)

Uranus (YUR-uh-nuhs)

Zeus (ZOOS)

Greek Towns, Regions, and Geography

Aegean (ih-JEE-uhn) Sea

Cephalonia (sehf-uh-LOH-nee-uh)

Constantinople (kahn-stant-uhn-OH-pahl)

Corfu (kohr-FOO)

Crete (KREET)

Cyclades (SIHK-luh-deez) Islands

Dodocanese (doh-DEHK-uh-neez) Islands

Epidaurus (ehp-uh-DAWR-uhs)

Epirus (ih-PY-ruhs)

Euboea (yu-BEE-uh)

Ionian (eye-OH-nee-uhn) Sea

Macedonia (mas-uh-DOH-nee-uh)

Monoclissia (mah-noh-klee-SEE-uh)

Peloponnesus (pehl-uh-puh-NEE-suhs)

Philippi (FIHL-uh-py)

Pilion (PEE-lee-uhn)

Piraeus (py-RAY-uhs)

Salonika (suh-LAHN-ih-kuh)

Souli (SOO-lee)

Thessaly (THEHS-uh-lee)

Thrace (THRAYS)

Volos (VOH-lahs)

Zante (ZAHN-teh)

Glossary

Acropolis (uh·KROP·oh·lihs)—the flat-topped hill in Athens where the Parthenon and other temples were built

agora (ag·ohr·AH)—the international open-air marketplace of ancient Athens

Argonauts (AHR·goh·nahts)—a legendary band of men who sailed with the hero Jason in search of the Golden Fleece

baklava (bahk·lah·VAH)—pastry made from thin layers of flaky dough, walnuts, and honey

bouzouki (boo·ZOO·kee)—popular Greek music that often deals with love; takes its name from a mandolin-like musical instrument

bouzoukia (boo·ZOO·kee·uh)—nightclubs where bouzouki music is played

Byzantine (BIHZ·uhn·teen) **Empire**—an offshoot of the Holy Roman Empire that ruled Greece for 1,100 years

chriso mou (hree·SOH MOO)—"my golden one"; used as a phrase of affection

christopsomo (hree·STOH·psoh·moh)—sweetened, decorated bread eaten in Greece at Christmastime

chronia polla (HROH·nee·ah poh·LAH)—"many years"; a phrase used to wish someone luck

city-state—a state which is made up of a city and its surrounding territory; created by the ancient Greeks

demotiki (dee·moh·tee·KEE) **music**—Greek folk music

dolmathes (dohl·MAH·thehz)—grape leaves stuffed with meat and rice

Epiphany (ee·PIH·fuh·nee)—a celebration in honor of the baptism of Christ

Erotokritos (eh·roh·TOH·kree·tohs)—a long epic poem about the Greek island of Crete and its history

fassolatha (fah·soh·LAH·thah)—bean soup; it can be eaten hot or cold

feta (FEH·tuh)—a cheese made from goats' milk

galatoboureko (gah·lah·toh·BOO·ree·koh)—a dessert made with custard and thin layers of flaky dough

gymnasio (gihm·NAH·zee·oh)—middle school, grades 7 through 9

idiotes (ih·dee·OH·tehz)—the ancient Athenian word used to describe citizens who did not participate in government

kafenion (kah·feh·NEE·ahn)—a Greek coffeehouse

kalanda (KAH·lahn·dah)—Christmas carols

kali orexi (kah·LEE OH·reh·ksee)—"good appetite"; a wish for an enjoyable meal

Kalikantzari (Kah·lee·KAHN·zah·ree)—legendary band of Christmas imps

Karagiozi (kah·rah·gih·OH·SEE)—a traditional shadow-puppet character; also the name of the theater where the puppet play is performed

kasseri (kah·SEH·ree)—a mild Greek cheese

klephtes (KLEHF·tehs)—patriot-warriors who rebelled against the Turkish authorities and were among the leaders of the War of Independence

liekey (leye·eh·KEE)—an open-air market

loukoumi (loo·KOO·mih)—a soft, chewy Greek candy

lykeion (LEE·kee·ohn)—senior high school; in Greece, there are two kinds: one gives students technical training, the other prepares students for college

Mantinades (mahn·TEE·nah·thehs)—a poem from Crete made up of many two-lined rhymes about Crete

matia mou (MAH·teeah MOO)—"my eyes"; a phrase of affection

mayeritsa (mah·yeh·REET·sah)—a soup made of egg, lemon, rice, and lamb parts

Meteora (meh·TEH·oh·rah)—gigantic columns of rock that stand in northwestern Thessaly

moussaka (moo·sah·KA)—a dish made with eggplant and ground meat

Mycenaeans (my·suh·NEE·uhns)—a group of people that lived in an area called Mycenaea in ancient Greece

oligarchy (OHL·ih·gahr·key)—a government in which a very small, usually wealthy, group controls the people

oxi (oh·HEE)—"no"; also pronounced "ochi"

Panayia Evangelistria (pah·nah·YEE·ah eh·vahn·geh·LEE·tree·uh)—a church on the island of Tinos with a painting that is said to cause miracles

Parthenon (PAHR·theh·nahn)—a large, ancient temple to Athena that was the main symbol of Greece's Golden Age

pastitsio (pah·STY·tsee·oh)—a dish of baked macaroni and ground meat

paximathi (pah·ksee·MAH·thee)—a plain biscuit

peripato (peh·REE·pah·toh)—the traditional evening stroll in a Greek neighborhood or town

philotemo (fee·LOH·tee·moh)—a Greek's self-respect

Plaka (PLAH·kah)—an old, hilly neighborhood of Athens with many restaurants and nightclubs

portocalathes (pohr·toh·kah·LAH·thahz)—a popular orange drink

poulaki mou (poo·LAH·kee MOO)—"my little bird"; a phrase of affection

Seeyion kali patritha (see·YEE·ohn kah·LEE pah·TREE·thah)—"to your health and to our homeland"; a Greek toast

souvlaki (soo·VLAH·kee)—lamb grilled on a spit

tavernas (tah·VEHR·nahs)—simple, working-class restaurants

tsoureki (tsoo·REH·kee)—Easter bread baked with dyed, unshelled hardboiled eggs decorating its top

tzatziki (tzah·TZEE·kee)—a yoghurt and cucumber dip
vasilopeta (vah·sih·LOH·pee·tah)—a cake eaten on January 1, St. Basil's Day
xenos (KSEH·nohs)—"stranger" or "friend"
zacharoplasteions (zah·hah·rah·plah·STEE·ohns)—shops that sell sweets and pastries
Zolongo (zoh·LOHN·goh) **dance**—a folksong that honors a town of women who died rather than be conquered

Selected Bibliography

Daly, Rosemary. *The Athenians in the Classical Period.* New York: Coward McCann, 1969.

Elliott, Drossoula Vassiliou. *We Live in Greece.* New York: The Bookwright Press, 1984.

Green, Roger Lancelyn. *Ancient Greece.* New York: The John Day Company, 1969.

Hale, William Harlan. *Ancient Greece.* New York: American Heritage Press, 1970.

Hamilton, Edith. *Mythology.* New York: New American Library, 1940.

Lyle, Garry. *Let's Visit Greece.* Bridgeport, Conn.: Burke Publishers, 1983.

Woodhouse, C. M. *Modern Greece.* London: Faber & Faber Limited, 1984.

Index

About the Author

As a first-generation American, Diana Spyropulos came to know Greece at an early age. She first visited Greece as a teenaged tourist, but later lived in Athens for two years. The time she spent in Greece, she says, "gave me valuable insights into many facets of Greek life." She has since gone back to Greece many times, most recently to complete the research for this book. Through *Greece: A Spirited Independence*, Spyropulos hopes to encourage young readers to develop an interest in both ancient Greece and the Greece of today.

Ms. Spyropulos is a free-lance writer and songwriter. She has published poems and short stories, acted on stage, narrated a film, and had many of her songs performed on radio, television, and in nightclubs. She has also taught English as a second language and creative writing. Spyropulos currently lives in Katonah, New York, with her two children.